HOW TO SLAY
THE Buffy WAY

HOW TO SLAY THE Buffy WAY

Badass Buffy Attitude and Killer Advice

DEY ST.
An Imprint of WILLIAM MORROW

Every girl who could have the power, will have the power.

Can stand up, will stand up.

Slayers every one of us.

Make your choice.

Are you ready to be strong?

BUFFY

EPISODE 22, SEASON 7

Being Brave and Badass

For as long as there
have been vampires,
there has been the Slayer.
One girl in all the world,
a Chosen One ...

——— *GILES*

He loves doing this part.

———
BUFFY

Episode 2, Season 1

I'm the thing that monsters have nightmares about.

BUFFY

Episode 11, Season 7

Thank god we're hot chicks with superpowers.

FAITH

Episode 21, Season 7

SO ARE YOU GOING TO KILL ME, OR ARE WE JUST MAKING SMALL ☕ TALK?

BUFFY

Episode 1, Season 2

No weapons, no friends,
no hope. Take all that
away and what's left?

———————————

ANGELUS

Me. ✝

———————————

BUFFY

Episode 21, Season 2

I laugh in the face of danger. Then I hide until it goes away.

XANDER

Episode 3, Season 1

Power.
I have it.
They don't.
This bothers them.

BUFFY

EPISODE 12, SEASON 5

MAYBE IF I COULD LEARN TO CONTROL THIS THING I COULD BE STRONGER, I COULD BE BETTER. BUT I'M SCARED.

BUFFY

EPISODE 1, SEASON 5

Maybe it's because of all the horrific things we've seen, but hippos wearing tutus just don't unnerve me the way they used to.

OZ

Episode 4, Season 4

I may be dead, but I'm still pretty.

BUFFY

Episode 12, Season 1

You're scared? That's smart.

You got questions? You should.

XANDER

Episode 18, Season 7

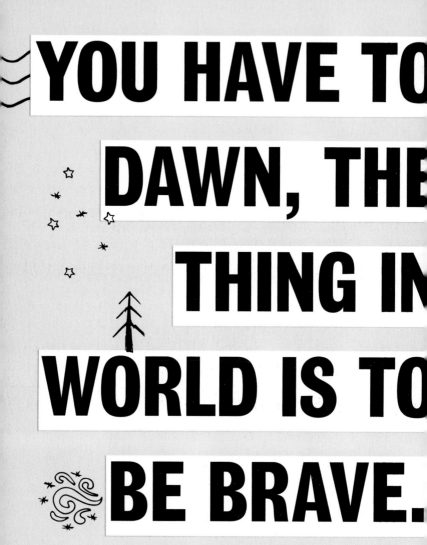

YOU HAVE TO DAWN, THE THING IN WORLD IS TO BE BRAVE.

BE STRONG.

HARDEST

HIS

IVE IN IT.

IVE.

BUFFY

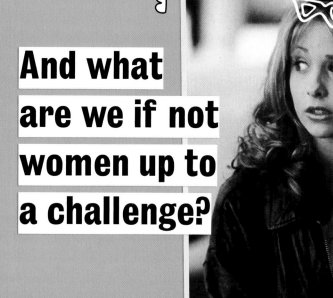

And what are we if not women up to a challenge?

BUFFY

Exactly. I mean, did we not put the 'GRR' in 'GIRL'?

WILLOW

EPISODE 2, SEASON 4

You wanna surprise the enemy?

Surprise yourselves.

Force yourself to do what can't be done.

BUFFY

Episode 15, Season 7

Mist.
Cemetery.
Halloween.

Should end well.

GILES

EPISODE 6, SEASON 6

Saving

the

World

I SUDDENLY FIND
MYSELF NEEDING TO
KNOW THE PLURAL
OF 'APOCALYPSE'.

———

RILEY

Episode 12, Season 4

I'm not exactly quaking in my stylish-yet-affordable boots but there's definitely something unnatural going on here, and that doesn't normally lead to hugs and puppies.

BUFFY

Episode 7, Season 6

I would love to be
upstairs, watching
TV or gossiping about
boys or even studying!

But I have to save the world.

Again.

Episode 21, Season 2

If you save the world I'll come back, we'll have drinks.

When! When, I mean.

CLEM

But the world continues to turn.

GILES

No one will ever know how close it came to stopping. Never know what we did.

WILLOW

Episode 13, Season 3

'Destroyer of the universe'. Guess cutting school doesn't seem so bad now, huh?

DAWN

Episode 20, Season 5

IF
APOCA
COMES,

Episode 5, Season 1

THE

YPSE

BEEP ME.

~~~~~~~~~~ BUFFY ~~~~~~~~~~

THEY THINK WE'RE GONNA WAIT FOR  THE END TO COME, LIKE WE ALWAYS DO.

I'M DONE WAITING.

THEY WANT AN ✝ APOCALYPSE?

WELL, WE'LL GIVE 'EM ONE.

BUFFY

EPISODE 10, SEASON 7

We saved the world.

I say we party.

BUFFY

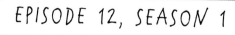

EPISODE 12, SEASON 1

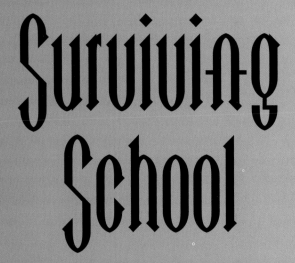

Surviving School

EPISODE 22, SEASON 2

CONGRATULATIONS TO THE 🏆 CLASS OF 1999. YOU ALL PROVED MORE OR LESS ADEQUATE. THIS IS A TIME OF CELEBRATION. SO SIT STILL AND BE QUIET.

PRINCIPAL SNYDER

The dead rose! We should at least have an assembly!

XANDER

Episode 2, Season 1

I know. If you don't go
out it'll be the end of
the world. Everything is
life or death when you're
a 16-year-old girl.

———

JOYCE

Episode 2, Season 1

Groping in a broom closet isn't dating. You don't call it a date until the guy spends money.

CORDELIA

We're proud to say the class of '99 has the lowest mortality rate of any graduating class in Sunnydale's history.

JONATHAN

Prom speech, Episode 20, Season 3

How was school today?

BUFFY

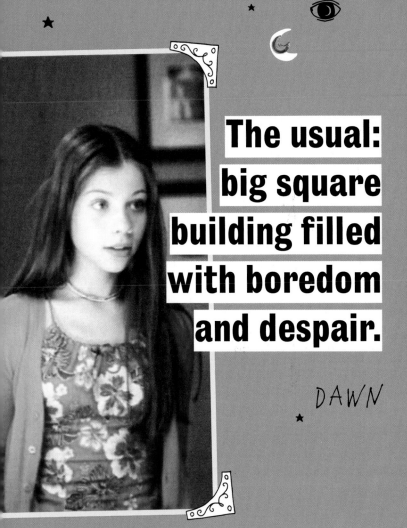

The usual: big square building filled with boredom and despair.

DAWN

EPISODE 13, SEASON 5

Giles lived for school. He's actually still bitter that there are only twelve grades.

 XANDER

Episode 8, Season 2

Sweetie, you wouldn't blow off a class if your head was on fire.

___

TARA

Episode 19, Series 5

You're really campaigning for bitch 👄 of the year, aren't you?

CORDELIA

As defending champion, you nervous?

BUFFY

I have witnessed a
millennium of treachery
and oppression from
the males of the species
and I have nothing but
contempt for the whole
libidinous lot of them.

ANYA

So why are you
talking to me?

XANDER

I don't have a
date for prom.

ANYA

Episode 20, Season 3

Guys. Take a moment to deal with all this. We survived.

OZ

It was a hell of a battle.

BUFFY

Not the battle.
High school.

OZ

Falling
in
Love

Episode 6, Season 2

Dates are things normal
girls have, who have
🕯 time to think about
nail polish and facials.
You know what I think about?

　◇　Ambush tactics.
◇ ◇✦ ◇ Beheading.

BUFFY

So you're feeling better about Angel?

WILLOW

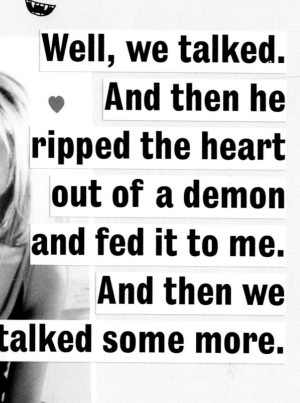

Well, we talked. And then he ripped the heart out of a demon and fed it to me. And then we talked some more.

BUFFY

EPISODE 18, SEASON 3

It used to be simple.

A hundred years,
just hanging out,
feeling guilty;
it really honed
my brooding
skills.

Then she comes along.

ANGEL

If you don't wanna fight, you don't fight. You don't use magic to make the fight go away.

TARA

Episode 8, Season 6

Anya, this is crazy.
We had a little fight.
That just means that
we have to work our way
through some stuff.
It doesn't mean we rebound
with the undead! 👁️‍👁️

———

XANDER

Episode 7, Season 6

The day you suss out what you do want, there'll probably be a parade.

SPIKE

YOU THINK HE'S TOO OLD BECAUSE HE'S A SENIOR? PLEASE!  MY BOYFRIEND HAD A BICENTENNIAL.

BUFFY

EPISODE 13, SEASON 2

A vampire in love with a slayer.

It's rather poetic.

In a maudlin sort of way.

GIVLES

Episode 11, Season 1

Are you mad at me for being around too much, or for not being around enough?

ANGEL

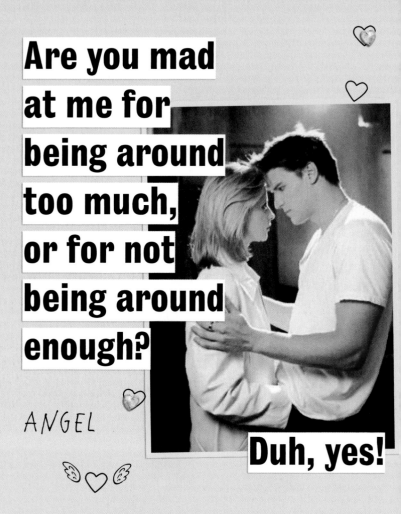

Duh, yes!

BUFFY

EPISODE 21, SEASON 3

Why waste time being all shy and worried about some guy and if he's going to laugh at you? Seize the moment.

Because tomorrow you might be dead.

BUFFY

Episode 1, Season 1

She wouldn't even kill me.
She just left.
She didn't even care enough
to cut off my head or
set me on fire.

Is that too much to ask?
You know, a little sign that
she cares?

_____

SPIKE

Episode 8, Season 3

Men can be such jerks sometimes.

Dead or alive.

WILLOW

EPISODE 17, SEASON 2

Without passion we'd be ❤ truly dead.

ANGEL

Episode 17, Season 2

Do you know what the saddest thing in the world is?

———

DARLA

Bad hair on top of that outfit?

———

BUFFY

To love someone who used to love you.

———

DARLA

Episode 7, Season 1

I've seen your kindness, and your strength, I've seen the best and the worst of you and I understand with perfect clarity exactly what you are.

You're a hell
of a woman.
You're the
one, Buffy.

—

SPIKE

Episode 20, Season 7

I LOVE YOU. NOTHING CAN CHANGE THAT, NOT EVEN DEATH.

ANGEL

EPISODE 13, SEASON 3

I know you'll never love me.
I'm a monster.
But you treat me like a man.

˅˄˅˅˅˅˅ ˅˅ SPIKE ˅˅˅˅˅˅˅ ˅˅

Episode 22, Season 5

Fighting Your Demons

Death is on your heels baby and sooner or later it's going to catch you.

EPISODE 7, SEASON 5

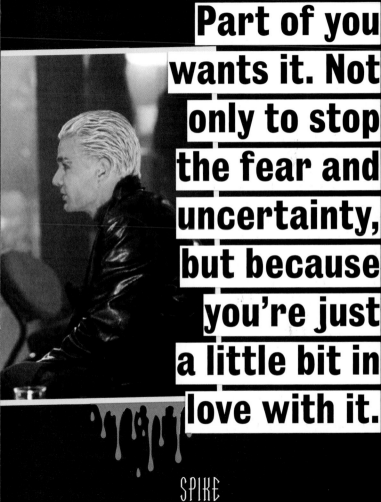

Part of you wants it. Not only to stop the fear and uncertainty, but because you're just a little bit in love with it.

SPIKE

To kill without remorse is to feel like a god.

❦ ANGEL ❧

Episode 15, Season 3

Look, we don't want trouble, you don't want trouble.

_____

WILLOW

Actually we do want trouble. We're demons. We're pretty much all about trouble.

_____

DEMON

Episode 2, Season 6

You have a plan?

GILES

I am the plan.

BUFFY

Episode 7, Season 4

People ... They're not even animals, they're just meatbag slaves to hormones, pheromones and their feelings.

GLORY

EPISODE 21, SEASON 5

Vampires are creeps.

BUFFY

Yes, that's why one slays them.

GILES

EPISODE 11, SEASON 2

I've sworn to protect this scary world, and sometimes that means saying and doing what other people can't.

They shouldn't have to.

GILES

Episode 22, Season 5

This is my lucky stake.

I have killed many vampires with it.

I call it 'Mr Pointy'.

KENDRA

Episode 20, Season 2

I FEEL LIKE STAYING IN. AND DOING MY HOMEWORK. AND FLOSSING. AND DYING A VIRGIN.

WILLOW

Episode 16, Season 3

Oh poor Watcher. Did your life pass before your eyes?

Cup of tea, cup of tea, almost got shagged, cup of tea ...

SPIKE

EPISODE 1, SEASON 6

Looking Out for Your Friends

I know you're about to do something apocalyptically evil and stupid, but hey, I still want to hang.

XANDER

EPISODE 22, SEASON 6

If it's guilt you're looking for Buffy, I'm not your man. All you will get from me is my support.

And my respect.

_____

GILES

Episode 14, Season 2

Things fall apart, Buffy.
And evil – it comes and goes.

But the way people manage is
that they don't do it alone.

They pull each other through.

Episode 11, Season 4

Whatever you choose, you've got my support.

Just think of me as … as your … You know, ⌣ **I'm searching for supportive things and I'm coming up all bras.**

XANDER

To forgive is an act
of compassion, Buffy.
It's not done because
people deserve it.

———

GILES

Episode 19, Season 2

You're not friends,
you'll never be friends.

You'll be in love till
it kills you both.

You'll fight and you'll shag
and you'll hate each other
until it makes you quiver.

But you'll never be friends.

SPIKE

Episode 8, Season 3

I just didn't want to put you in that kind of danger.

BUFFY

As opposed to the other kind we're always in?

XANDER

~~~~~ EPISODE 13, SEASON 5 ~~~~~

Finding
Your
Way

STRONG IS

IT'S HARD,

PAINFUL

EVERY DAY,

WE HAVE

Episode 10, Season 3

FIGHTING. AND IT'S AND IT'S IT'S WHAT TO DO.

BUFFY

It's because you don't have a strong father figure, isn't it?

JOYCE

It's just fate, Mom. I am the Slayer. Accept it.

BUFFY

Episode 21, Season 2

It's terribly simple. The good guys are always stalwart and true. The bad guys are easily distinguished by their pointy horns or black hats. We always defeat them and save the day.

GILES

Liar.

BUFFY

Episode 7, Season 2

You're not special, you're extraordinary.

XANDER

Episode 12, Season 7

I'm way cooler than you are
👓 'cause I'm not a sheep.
I do what I wanna do, and
I wear what I wanna wear.
And you know what?
I'll date whoever the hell
I wanna date.

No matter how lame he is.

CORDELIA

Something made us different.
We're warriors, we're built to kill.

FAITH

Kill demons! But it doesn't mean
we get to pass judgement, like
we're better than everyone else.

BUFFY

Episode 15, Season 3

In the end, we all are who we are, no matter how much we may appear to have changed.

GILES

Episode 1, Season 7

I GOT IT SO WRONG.
I DON'T WANNA
PROTECT YOU FROM
THE WORLD.

I WANNA SHOW
IT TO YOU.

BUFFY

Episode 22, Season 6

The big moments are gonna come. You can't help that. It's what you do afterwards that counts.

That's when you find out who you are.

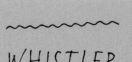

WHISTLER

EPISODE 21, SEASON 2

I don't know how to live in this world if these are the choices.

BUFFY

Episode 22, Season 5

FUNNY HOW THE EARTH NEVER OPENS UP AND SWALLOWS YOU WHEN YOU WANT IT TO.

XANDER

EPISODE 4, SEASON 1

Sometimes the most
adult thing you can
do is ask for help
when you need it.

〰〰〰〰〰

GILES

Episode 22, Season 6

Time was, I thought humans existed just to hurt each other. Then I came here and found out that there are other types of people. People who genuinely want to do right. ☆ Then they make mistakes, they fall down, but they keep trying.

ANGEL

Episode 15, Season 3

Nothing's ever simple any more. I'm constantly trying to work it out – who to love or hate, who to trust. It's just like, the more I know the more confused I get.

BUFFY

I believe that's called growing up.

GILES

Episode 7, Season 2

I MAKE IT THROUGH THIS AND THE NEXT THING AND THE NEXT THING, AND MAYBE ONE DAY I TURN AROUND AND REALISE I'M READY.

BUFFY

EPISODE 22, SEASON 7

DEY ST.

HarperCollins books may be purchased for educational, business, or sales promotional use. For information, please email the Special Markets Department at SPsales@harpercollins.com.

Published in the UK in 2018 by Ebury Press/Penguin Random House

FIRST U.S. EDITION

Library of Congress Cataloging-in-Publication Data has been applied for.

ISBN 978-0-06-289582-0

18 19 20 21 22 LSC 10 9 8 7 6 5 4 3 2 1